A Women's Guide To Spiritual Warfare

Family spiritual Warfare Books

Johannes Tefo

Published by Johannes Tefo, 2023.

Also by Johannes Tefo

Family spiritual Warfare Books
Generational Curses And Spiritual Warfare: Spiritual Strategies & Principles Of Victory Against Evil Strongholds
Youth's Guide To Spiritual Warfare
A Women's Guide To Spiritual Warfare

Standalone
Deliver Your Soul From Evil
Overcoming Spirit Of Stagnation
The 24: Prophetic Word For This Season 2024 And Beyond
Michael For Warfare
Territorial Spirits: Overcome Evil Strongholds in Your Life And Take Over Your Community With Strategic Warfare And Winning Prayers
Prayers Against Suicide Spirit
Spiritual Warfare When Enough is Enough
Identity In Christ
Prayers Against Satanic Networks

The Workplace You Need: Spiritual Warfare Prayers That Silence Evil Powers At Your Workplace.

Deliverance From Mind Control: Be Free And Delivered From Every Marine Demons Of Mind Control

Times Getting Hard: Scriptures Of Comfort For Hard Days

Battle In The Sea: How To Tackle Spiritual Warfare And Win The Battle

Freedom: Deliverance Of Souls From Captivity

A Dedicated Prayer Lifestyle: Simple Tips To Effective Prayer Lifestyle

Deliverance From Sexual Dreams

Sexual Lust, Demons, And Impurity

Redefined By Fire: Unleashing The Power Of The Holy Spirit Within.

Table of Contents

Dedicated to women all over the world, God loves you and believes in you. Walk tall, honor the good Lord. All shall be well.

Preface.

Miracles happens every day. It is a miracle to live. If we all have to testify about the goodness of the Lord—every breath of every being will declare His marvellous works about the power of his word. If it wasn't for the Lord—I wouldn't be writing this message to you. This message is inspired by the wonders God is performing in my life. He is certainly doing the same to you. But at the end of the day, we partner with God through faith. With faith all things are possible. If you want to wow Christ and the cloud of witness—exercise faith!

Faith as small as mustard seeds moves mountains. We activate faith through our mouth. Our mouth is one of the valuable assets in this kingdom business. I'm totally healed from schizophrenia through the power of the Word. Survived and thrived in a haunted house. I have seen the hand of the Living God in my life, God shielding me from the power of witchcraft and occult.

Had encounter with the Devil. Had encounter with marine kingdom, and prevailed by the grace of the name of God of Jacob—my defender. Had encounter with the dragon—leviathan in my village. Fought with gods of this world—and prevailed. Christ is the king. If you want to see the kingship of Christ, have faith in God. Neglect not his word. The precepts of the holy bible are path to life forever more.

There have been numerous times whereby I died and came back to life. In the year 2017 to 2018, I went near-death experience through consumption of poisonous substance. I Spend two weeks in hospital. This experience marked my first real encounter with the Living God. I am a prophet; God has always been speaking to me but that one encounter was radical. I have to tell you that, the best gift in this life, is to live a prayerful life. Live every day of your life for God.

So far I have written a lot of books about spiritual warfare merely because I believe if you are going to take your position in the land of your promise, you are going to fight for what is yours. It is a thin line between light and darkness. But light always prevails. If you admire to move in ranks and reach new height in spirit—be a warrior in spirit! Fight the good fight. We have numerous weapons to dismantle the kingdom of the enemy. Then we shall inherit the wealth of the heathen.

The bible is your most recent weapon in this day and age, just like Moses rod in exodus. The man of God, Moses, was commissioned to deliver the army of God from the hand of Pharaoh. He wrought miraculous works that even today no one dares to challenge through the strong arm of the Lord. Even in this day, the word of God is equivalent to that Moses's rod to move mountains. The arm of the Lord is still strong and still high above all the nations. Proclaim the word, confess the word, and you shall reap the rewards of the word. The best prayers are scriptural prayers. God values this kinds of prayers because they speak His will. Pray the will of God.

Proverb 18:20-21 A man's belly shall be satisfied with the fruit of his mouth; and with the increase of his lips shall he be filled. 21 Death and life are in the power of the tongue: and they that love it shall eat the fruit thereof.

Man is justified by his words—and he also shall be judgement by his words. This statement tells it like it is. I remember going through territorial attacks while I was engaging in a territorial warfare, and I saw a very huge principal demon just staring at me as if it is waiting for me to say something—and the spirit of the Lord told me that I should be careful of what I say and what I think. That demon was to going to snare me through my speech. In the realm of spirit or in the spirit world, words travel in speed within space and time. Words are more powerful than diamonds and pearls. Not only words, but your thoughts as well. You always have to renew your mind with the word of God. Think good thoughts that are pure, holy and worthy because the enemy is waiting for an opportunity to get in through filthy thoughts.

Brethren, we can change the atmosphere of our lives if we can live a life fully dedicated to the will of God. Like if you think of doing something, ask yourself this question "I am I glorifying the Lord with this?" This will change your perception on many things. We do wrong things becomes of the influence of media and culture. Especially we as the body of Christ, the believer in the Lord, we allow the church culture to dictate us how to live our lives while it should be the word and spirit of God directing us. Some of the traditions are man-made.

Psalm 19:7-8 The law of the LORD is perfect, converting the soul: the testimony of the LORD is sure, making wise the simple. 8 The statutes of the LORD are right, rejoicing the heart: the commandment of the LORD is pure, enlightening the eyes.

The perfect and undiluted law will direct us to the correct destination. Every scripture testifies about the goodness of the Lord. You can never go wrong exalting your Maker. It is written that He inhabits the praises of Israel.

Chapter 1-Blessing or curse

The is no beautiful feeling than a feeling of being free from something.

"For I, the Lord your God, am a jealous God, punishing the children for the sin of the fathers to the third and fourth generation of those who hate me, but showing love to a thousand generations of those who love me and keep my commandments" (Ex. 20:5-6).

Freedom is precious. Especially when you been tossed and turned around. This is what a life of curse does to many of us. You can truly know when you add two and two—and when it does not add up. The cycle of going around the bush when you are about to receive breakthrough. I always tell people that, when you going through the most in a season, what you are about to reap is bigger than you. That's why the enemy is working overtime to abort the dream.

It is actually a set time where you have to be stubborn in faith—and never let it go. All kinds of faith go. All kinds of prayers go. I remember when I was going through witchcraft attacks, the holy spirit inspired me that all kinds of prayers go. You never know which one of the weaponry weapon from the hand of God shall set you free. Above all, faith determines how far you can go.

We cannot talk about faith and not talk about the hall of famers of Hebrew 11—Abraham, Moses, Elijah, and others. God honors faith. People are going to talk about these men even ages to come. When you believe in the Lord God of host, He will have you making impact even when you are gone. Your memory will last forever. The upright in heart are close to God. Right standing with our Maker is the only way of life of peace and content.

The opposite cries, a life of cursed, is a life of the absence of God 'blessings in your life. Sin is when you are rebellious—harkening not to the voice of God about a way of life He has set for you to walk on. When you read Deuteronomy 28, you find that it is all about listening to God and listening not to God. Blessings are bestowed upon those who listen to God—and curses falls upon those who do not. Who you listen to is very important.

The counsel of the holy spirit leads you on the good path filled with great promises of God and peace of mind. A fellowship with spirit of Christ is life of complete.

Spirit of the Lord brings liberty. While other spirit brings confusion. Life of curse is a life of confusion. You don't know what to do when things get out of hands. People look down at you as if you do not belong or exists, you feel overwhelmed—and sense of hopelessness keeps on creeping in. That is not how a life of a believer supposed to be.

Through my study and experience, I found that majority of people suffer for the things that they did not even have their hands on. It is the consequences of the sins of their forefathers. By merely forgetting God and indulging with other gods ultimately create a gateway for familiar demons to enter into the house and start to act as strongman or strongwomen of that house. Heredity sins have impact on your life than you think. It is by the grace, mercy and truth of the Living God that is leading us out of the dunghill.

This is a hot topic whereby some preachers and ministers of the gospel believes that a Christian cannot be cursed and cannot have a demon. Christ worked wonders in the life of Israelites, healing and delivering them from all their infirmities. These were the people of faith under the covenant of Moses. These people were believers and had faith in the one true God of Jesus.

I strongly believe and without a doubt that, generational curses are strongholds and serve as barriers within our respected family for not to fully delivered in aspects of our lives. Some are stagnant, unemployed, barren, idol worshipping, prostituting etc. All due to strongman our forefathers have conjured up, some knowing, while some unaware of the consequences thereafter.

Deuteronomy 28:1-14

1 And it shall come to pass, if thou shalt hearken diligently unto the voice of

the LORD thy God, to observe and to do all his commandments which I

command thee this day, that the LORD thy God will set thee on high above all nations of the earth: 2 And all these blessings shall come on thee, and overtake

thee, if thou shalt hearken unto the voice of the LORD thy God.

3 Blessed shalt thou be in the city, and blessed shalt thou be in the field.

4 Blessed shall be the fruit of thy body, and the fruit of thy ground, and the

fruit of thy cattle, the increase of thy kine, and the flocks of thy sheep.

5 Blessed shall be thy basket and thy store.

6 Blessed shalt thou be when thou comest in, and blessed shalt thou be

when thou goest out.

7 The LORD shall cause thine enemies that rise up against thee to be

smitten before thy face: they shall come out against thee one way, and flee

before thee seven ways.

8 The LORD shall command the blessing upon thee in thy storehouses, and

in all that thou settest thine hand unto; and he shall bless thee in the land which

the LORD thy God giveth thee.

9 The LORD shall establish thee an holy people unto himself, as he hath

sworn unto thee, if thou shalt keep the commandments of the LORD thy God,

and walk in his ways.

10 And all people of the earth shall see that thou art called by the name of
the LORD; and they shall be afraid of thee.
11 And the LORD shall make thee plenteous in goods, in the fruit of thy
body, and in the fruit of thy cattle, and in the fruit of thy ground, in the land
which the LORD sware unto thy fathers to give thee.
12 The LORD shall open unto thee his good treasure, the heaven to give the
rain unto thy land in his season, and to bless all the work of thine hand: and thou
shalt lend unto many nations, and thou shalt not borrow.
13 And the LORD shall make thee the head, and not the tail; and thou shalt
be above only, and thou shalt not be beneath; if that thou hearken unto the
commandments of the LORD thy God, which I command thee this day, to
observe and to do them: 14 And thou shalt not go aside from any of the words
which I command thee this day, to the right hand, or to the left, to go after other
gods to serve them.

Cheer up, for Christ has triumphed. It is through his precious blood that we are atoned. He is our Passover lamb. He has become a curse for you so that you can be blessed. The victory of Christ has afforded you power to walk in dominion in every area of your life to command the spirits of the house of your fathers to go.

Galatians 3:13-14 Christ hath redeemed us from the curse of the law, being made a curse for us: for it is written, Cursed is every one that hangeth on a tree:

14 That the blessing of Abraham might come on the Gentiles through Jesus

Christ; that we might receive the promise of the Spirit through faith.

Total deliverance from God means that you shall be above not beneath. You shall be the head not the tail. You shall be prosperous in your undertakings. The opposite of these, call your life to be examined. However, not all poverty means you are cursed or bewitched. But if it is prolonged, then there is a need for deliverance.

Psalm 112:3 Wealth and riches shall be in his house: and his righteousness endureth for

ever.

Wealth and riches are promises for you. Over the past years, the church has made it look like it is a bad thing for child of God to be wealthy or rich. There is nothing wrong with wealth. It is even a good thing to advance the kingdom of God when the Lord God has blessed you. For all I know, Abraham was blessed, Isaac was blessed and Jacob also. There is no glory in poverty. It is out of the abundance heart of God to bless you and makes you walk tall and high.

Psalm 91:16 With long life will I satisfy him, and show him my salvation.

It cannot be a long life of misery and sorrow but of satisfying life and deliverance from all kinds of things.

Psalm 92:12-14 The righteous shall flourish like the palm tree: he shall grow like a cedar in Lebanon. 13 Those that be planted in the house of the LORD shall flourish in the courts of our God. 14 They shall still bring forth fruit in old age; they shall be fat and flourishing;

Agreeing in faith in God will have you reaping good benefits even in old age. This is a blessedth life.

Psalm 93:1 The LORD reigneth, he is clothed with majesty; the LORD is clothed with strength, wherewith he hath girded himself: the world also is stablished, that it cannot be moved.

Repenting of the sins of our forefathers will drive away all evil stronghold over our families. All the divisions, hurts, jealousy and hate we see in family will be subdued. Behind every personality there is spirit. It all start off with act of humility. By surrendering our will before the Marker of the universe.

"Christ redeemed us from the curse of the law by becoming a curse for us, for it is written: 'Cursed is everyone who is hung on a tree,'" Galatians 3:13

"I have set before you life and death, blessings and curses. Now choose life, so that you and your children may live," Deuteronomy 30:19

"If my people who are called by my name, will humble themselves and pray and seek my face and turn from their wicked ways then I will hear from heaven and will forgive their sin and I will heal their land," 2 Chronicles 7: 14

Identifying curses and breaking them

The first step to freedom is to identify curses in your life, be it personal curses, generational curses and family curse lurking in your bloodline. There has never been a perfect time to redeem your bloodline than now.

The patterns in your family may give you enough clue for what to fight. In my family line there has never been someone who passed the age of 70, even from the traced lineage from back to 3 to 4 generations. And many of my people died due to food poisoning, some men through alcohol consumption. Looking at the pattern of their death—I can tell that the spirit of untimely death is at work. While majority of them where quite living a good life, some having good financial status but they died poor eventually. These are some of the family patterns to look at when you are identifying curses and in the process of breaking them.

As a spiritual warfare warrior, you stand at the gate of your life, your family and community as a watcher. Prophet Ezekiel stood as the watcher in Jerusalem. A watcher is a seer who go in the realm of spirit to observe the roots of the matter and what is actually going on in any prophetic matter. You might not be in the office of the prophet but the spirit of the Living God in you grant you access to prophetic office.

God will take you on the spiritual journey to see what is the course of some of your problem you are facing in your life. Because some of you, your life has even been negotiated in the realm of the spirit by your forefathers. You will find that before you were even conceived, your parents have made covenant with some spirits for you to be born. Especially in Africa, many have gone to traditional healers to conceive. And as the results, spirits have to be summoned in the process. And sadly, these are not good spirit to tamper with. This is the marine kingdom that is robbing the destinies of many man and women all over the world.

Simply, generational curse is any ailment of the mind, body, and spirit resulting from negative behavioral patterns that are passed down throughout several generations. Some examples of generational curses are: addictions (i.e. drug/alcohol, sex), mental illnesses (depression, schizophrenia, bipolar depression), physical illnesses (hypertension, heart disease, cancer), and even poverty to name a few. It is ideal to understand the origin and dimensions of a to generational curse and destroy it completely.

That's when fasting and praying should come handy to deal with these issues because some of the problem cannot be defeated without fasting and praying. If you look at Mathews 17:21, you will realize that Christ mentioned that some demons can only to driven when we stand in unequivocal faith in God.

This scripture below testifies that some demons cannot go, and some healing cannot manifest except through prayer and fasting.

Mathews 17:15-21 Lord, have mercy on my son: for he is lunatick, and sore vexed: for

Often times he falleth into the fire, and oft into the water.

16 And I brought him to thy disciples, and they could not cure him.

17 Then Jesus answered and said, O faithless and perverse generation, how
long shall I be with you? how long shall I suffer you? bring him
hither to me.
18 And Jesus rebuked the devil; and he departed out of him:
and the child
was cured from that very hour.
19 Then came the disciples to Jesus apart, and said, Why could
not we cast
him out?
20 And Jesus said unto them, Because of your unbelief: for
verily I say unto
you, If ye have faith as a grain of mustard seed, ye shall say unto this mountain,
Remove hence to yonder place; and it shall remove; and nothing shall be
impossible unto you.
21 Howbeit this kind goeth not out but by prayer and fasting.
These are some of the curses that can stand between you and
your blessing or breakthrough.

✚ Sexual perversion includes adultery, fornication, incest, bestiality, homosexuality, lesbianism, oral sex, anal sex, orgies, molestation, and rape. A history of these sexual sins in the bloodline opens the door for Curses of Lust.

✚ Financial perversion includes the misuse of money, unjust gain, cheating, gambling, covetousness, not honoring God (by tithing), bribes, crooked means of obtaining money, illegal trafficking of drugs and alcohol, robbery, and embezzlement. A history of these sins in the bloodline can open the door for Curses of Poverty.

✣ Religious perversion includes idolatry, worshipping idols, ancestral worship, and oaths and pledges to idol gods. A history of these sins in the bloodline can open the door for the Curse of Idolatry and Multiple Curses.

✣ Spiritual perversion includes witchcraft, voodoo, sorcery, divination, occult involvement, and Spiritism. A history of these sins in the bloodline can open the door for Multiple Curses.

✣ Behavioral perversion includes a perverse way, pride, rebellion, drunkenness, murder, returning evil for good, sinful attitudes and ways, ungodly conduct, mistreating others, abuse, and unrighteous behavior.

✣ Familial perversion includes perversion of the family order, Ahab and Jezebel spirits (see 1 Kings 16-21), men not taking leadership, dominating females, rebellious children, or any time God's order in the family is violated and neglected. This perversion opens the door for Curses upon Marriages and Families.

✣ Perverse speech includes spoken curses, vexes, hexes, spells, lying, blasphemy, slander, crooked speech, vows, oaths and pledges to idols, cults, false gods, enchantments, and bewitchments.

Prayers to break any generational curses

Many people are exposed to living with the bondage of sins inherited from their forefathers. This can continue on for generations until repentance is sought. Here is a look at some great prayers for breaking generational curses that will help to put you on a path to heal any generational transgressions.

1. Redeemed from the Curse Prayer Father God, it is for freedom that Christ came; I am redeemed from the curse of the law. I stand firm in this verse, and I decree and declare that every generational curse in my lineage does not have power over me. Every curse spoken, written, or transferred to me is broken by the blood of Jesus. Poverty, sickness, and family idols are not my portion. I choose to walk in the freedom that Christ bought for me in the name of Jesus, Amen.

2. Confession Prayer Lord God, I come humbly before you today to confess the sins that my forefathers and I have committed against you. We have not obeyed your word, and as a result, has opened up doors for the devil to reinforce generational curses into our family, Father, forgive us of all. Let the blood of your son Jesus purify us from every sin that we have committed against you. Holy Spirit, purge every curse that has passed on in our family from generation to generation, in Jesus name I pray, Amen.

3. Agreements and Vows Prayer Lord, creator of heaven and earth, I thank you for sending your only son to die on the cross for us. Through his sacrifice, we have been set free from any manner of captivity. I break myself and my future generation from any agreements, vows, commitments, and contracts that my family and I made knowingly or unknowingly with the forces of darkness. Today, I renounce these agreements in the name of Jesus, and I declare that my family has been set free, in Jesus name, I pray, Amen.

4. Purification Prayer Lord Jesus, I want to thank you for dying on the cross for me. It is because of your great sacrifice that my family and I have been set free from generational curses. I break the power of the enemy over my life. I declare and decree that every curse that the enemy and his agents are trying to reinforce in my life is null and void. I paralyze all the works of the enemy over my life. I reject every curse in my family line and choose to walk in the blessings of Abraham. In the name of Jesus, I believe and pray, Amen.

5. Authority Prayer O Lord Jesus, the Bible says that I will decree a thing and it shall be established. I cancel and nullify any curses that were spoken over us intentionally or unintentionally in the name of Jesus. I cancel the effects of those negative words over my family and future generations in the name of Jesus. I declare and decree that generational curses of sickness, poverty, marital failure, bareness, rage, alcoholism, and lying are null and void. They will never manifest because we are free from them. I command the devil and his demons to leave my family alone in the name of Jesus.

6. New Creation Prayer Father, I thank you for making me a new creation in Christ. I choose to walk in my new found freedom in Christ. I refuse to be chained to generation curses from my parents'

house. I stand firm in my new Identity and declare that I am of a different bloodline line, and that is the bloodline of Jesus. Devil and your cohorts of demons, you have no power over my mental health, finances, family, and marriage because who the son has set free is free indeed. I am free in the name of Jesus, Amen.

7. Breaking the Curse of Sinful Patterns Prayer Lord Jesus, I renounce sinful patterns that have been going on in my family from generation to generation. I renounce sexual immorality, alcoholism, bitterness, gossip, and rage in my lineage. I cut myself off and break free from those sinful patterns in the name of Jesus. I plead the blood of Jesus Christ over myself, and I declare that those sinful patterns will not have a hold of me or any of my children and future generations. We belong to Christ, and therefore generational sins have no power over us in the mighty name of Jesus, I pray, Amen.

8. Breaking the Curse of Premature Death Prayer Heavenly Father, I want to thank you for removing me from the kingdom of darkness and transferring me into the kingdom of your son, Jesus. I belong to a new family now. You foul spirit of premature death that has been haunting my family for generations; I break your power over my life in the mighty name of Jesus. Devil, I remind you that I belong to a new family now. You have no control over my life. My family and I will live to declare the glorious works of the Lord in Jesus' name, Amen.

9. Breaking the Curse of Rejection Prayer Father in heaven, I come to your throne today to confess all my sins and the sins of my forefathers. Thank you for forgiving us of our past, present and future sins, and accepting us into your family. We have sinned against you, and as a result, our family has been under the curse of rejection. I break and loose myself from curses of rejection from my father's house in the name of Jesus. I declare that none of my children and grandchildren will be rejected because we now belong to your family. We shall always find favor with you and man in Jesus' name, I believe, and pray, Amen.

10. Blessing Prayer Father God, your word says that you have adopted me into your family. Therefore, I am Abraham's descendant and an heir, together with Christ. From today onwards, I refuse to walk in the curses of my family and choose to walk in the blessings of Abraham. I break free from every curse that has spoken over me by my family, friends, and even strangers. I cancel the power of predictions made over my life. I declare that I am a blessing to my loved ones and not a curse. The work of my hand is blessed. I am at the top, never at the bottom. I am blessed when I come in, and when I go out. In Jesus' name, I believe and pray, Amen.

Chapter 2-Remembering God

There is time to take a journey on the memory line about your life and how your Maker has been a strong tower over situations. Especially when you are on the rock bottom—it is ideal to reminisce of the ages of goodness the Lord God has been. This is what King David will do. Especially when you are in the wilderness, not knowing what to do and how to get out of that situation. As believers, we all know that there a season where God feels distant, no sign, no prophecy, nada. Even when He said He will never leave you—there are some time where you feel left alone. This statement is relatable to majority of prophets we come across in the bible. There is a time where one has to cry out psalm 22 "My God, my God why has you forsaken me".

Psalm 22:1 My God, my God, why hast thou forsaken me? why art thou so far from helping me, and from the words of my roaring?

The beautiful thing about our God is that He is closer that you think. His spirit is present than you think. And it not like you are walking in unrighteousness or anything. It just that there is time for everything under the sun. and the secrets things belongs to the Lord. There are sometimes where you fully have to trust the process and trust the God. Prophetess Deborah will write and sing victory songs over Israel before she even goes to war. The act of faith is displayed not when you got the results but by what you do in the process. Faith holds all things together.

Hebrew 11:6 But without faith it is impossible to please him: for he that cometh to God must believe that he is, and that he is a rewarder of them that diligently seek him.

You will see and realize that when you are under attack—the only thing that will keep you motivated and going is faith. I know there are various spiritual weapons you can tackle to win the fight but all of them require your earnest and heartfelt faith to conquer. It is faith that will make you a conqueror in this life. Whether in marriage, parenting, career or in self-development—faith will get you going to places you have never been.

It is literally easy as ABC to develop your faith. Remember, even childlike faith can do wondrous things. You read the word and make it connect to your situation. The best practical way is to start personalizing the word, meditate on, ponder on, until it is engraved in your soul. Your subconscious mind need at all time to be reminded that you can. God can. And you can. Because you are the child of the Most High God.

Psalm 82:6 I have said, Ye are gods; and all of you are children of the most High.

In spirit we are begot by the Most High. We resemble the Living Father in so much. The light of God and holy spirit that is within us help us connect with our Maker—the God of the universe. One thing that majority of us overlook is worship. Worship is the chain breaker, the demon slayer and the atmosphere changer. At the heart of sincere truth and act of worship—the heavens can inhabit the earth. I am sure your already heard of where God dwells.

Psalm 22:3 But thou art holy, O thou that inhabitest the praises of Israel.

Psalm 149:6 Let the high praises of God be in their mouth, and a twoedged sword in their hand; 7 To execute vengeance upon the heathen, and punishments upon the people;

When David woke early in the morning to sing to the Lord, he did not only sing during happy hours, he sang also in dark hours. Giving God all the glory is not like a button you just turn it on or off whenever you feel like. It is continuous. It is an ongoing and everlasting mission. I used to listen to Dion Warwick all-time best song titled *That's what friends are for*. And in the record she sings "in good times, in bad times, that's what friends are for". Make God your best friends for all the time you still breathing under the sun. He shall cover you, clothe you, honor you and do much more that what your friends and family can do put together.

You only need to raise the high praises unto the Father of all. Your two-edged sword is the word of God in your heart released through your mouth to silence all your enemies. The devil is your number one enemy and his hosts. As much as we call the Lord God, the Lord of Host, the Devil also has his host of demons aimed at you to distract you from your godly path. It is survival of the fittest—the evil is all around us but we have some dangerous deadly weapon to drive him out of our lives. You will see that I will touch on these weapons later. Folks, we are on the winning team by being on God' side. Since there are two side, its either you are with the devil or with Christ.

The truth be told though, you cannot just wake up one morning and found out that all your problems are gone. It is when we press into his glory—his unapproachable light that we are strengthened and revived by his spirit to soldier on. We are warriors and soldiers of the Lord of the armies. We are the army of the Lord for His kingdom on earth. Thy kingdom speeds up on earth when we kneel down in the honor of His name.

Chapter 3- Meditating on His goodness

You will wonder why I have included this chapter as a warfare tactic. However, meditating is what guarantee us success in the kingdom business. When you shift your eyes from your problem and focus on the BIG GOD you have—a new perspective arises in you. The lion and lioness in you start to roar more and more. The righteous are bold as lion. You shall be bold and walk your head lifted up—arising above your problems. Clearly speaking, many water arise to engulf us.

Psalm 69:1 Save me, O God; for the waters are come in unto my soul. 2 I sink in deep mire, where there is no standing: I am come into deep waters, where the floods overflow me.

Isaiah 43:2 When thou passest through the waters, I will be with thee; and through the rivers, they shall not overflow thee: when thou walkest through the fire, thou shalt not be burned; neither shall the flame kindle upon thee.

We are bound to find ourselves in hot waters or cold waters. But He promises to be with us just like He has been with Moses. Just as the Israelites passed the Red sea through the arm of the Living God—He shall lead you like shepherd. Your God is a great king—and a Man of War—that's why He is called the Lord God of Host.

You will recall that Shadrack, Meshach and Abednego were thrown in the fire and the presence of the God of heaven was with them in the fire. The angel of God protected these three Jewish men from the fire. But they went through the fire. After the fire is glory. Glory, honor and power comes after great tribulation. Look at Job, Daniel, Paul, Christ, Stephen etc. These men suffered than ordinary people—but God is the rewarder of those who diligently seek Him. Those who are zealous with the kingdom business like Elijah.

Psalm 69: 9 For the zeal of thine house hath eaten me up; and the reproaches of them

that reproached thee are fallen upon me.

The dark spirits of these world are on the mission to draw you away from your Creator. In Christ already you know who you are—don't let anything hold you down—reach your God given destiny through the grace of the Living God. It is a good thing when the zeal of the house of God eat you up.

Blessed are they that dwell in thy house: they will be still praising thee.

Selah.

5 Blessed is the man whose strength is in thee; in whose heart are the ways

of them (Psalm 84:4-5).

The beauty of His holiness is seen in his tabernacle. Apostle Paul raised the standard even high as he likens our body with the temple of God. The indwelling of the holy spirit within us give us access to reach the throne of God, no matter who you are, and no matter where you at. Spirit, soul and body resembles the temple of Solomon. You have the outer court, the inner court and the holy of holies. The holy of holies is the spot we ought to reach when we meditate and when we worship. This is the highest and deepest level you can tap into in the kingdom of God—especially in the prophetic.

Psalm 100:4-5 Enter into his gates with thanksgiving, and into his courts with praise: be
thankful unto him, and bless his name.
5 For the LORD is good; his mercy is everlasting; and his truth endureth to
all generations.

This psalm laid out the blueprint of accessing the presence of God in a simple manner. You will find pastors and prophets complicating things with method to reach new heights in the spirit to experience the glory of the Living God. This is the set time whereby we do not go up on the mountain to reach God's glory but call upon the glory of the God of Israel wherever we are. Moses climbed the mountaintop. Christ came down to dwell among us.

Psalm 22:3 But thou art holy, O thou that inhabitest the praises of Israel.

When you worship, praise or offer sacrifice of thanksgiving to the Most High, you are meditating on His character. And this build you up in spirit—and allows you to take off the garment of heaviness that have been tampering with our souls. Your precious soul has to connect with His Creator. For all souls belongs unto God.

Souls are revived by holy spirit that is within us. Souls are restored by God.

Psalms 147:3 He healeth the broken in heart, and bindeth up their wounds.

Psalms 23:3 He restoreth my soul: he leadeth me in the paths of righteousness for his

name's sake.

Throughout the bible, concerning faith, the word says fear not. Merely because fear is the opposite of faith. Scriptures will make sense and come life to you when ponder, think and utters of them. Joshua success rested on the idea of meditating on the word day and night—and obedience. Faith and obedience works together like ying and yang.

Psalm 1:2 But his delight is in the law of the LORD; and in his law doth he meditate

day and night.

Joshua 1:5 There shall not any man be able to stand before thee all the days of thy life: as I was with Moses, so I will be with thee: I will not fail thee, nor forsake thee.

Joshua 1:8 This book of the law shall not depart out of thy mouth; but thou shalt meditate therein day and night, that thou mayest observe to do according to all that is written therein: for then thou shalt make thy way prosperous, and then thou shalt have good success.

The word of God is alive and active sharper than a two-edged sword. The word already is ordained to judge, correct, reprove and do much more. Especially when you are filled with the Holy ghost, decreeing and declaring the word will make immediate impact to situations.

This law shall not depart in your mouth because the word in your mouth is power. As a women of God seated in heavenly places in Christ, already you seat in the position of dominion—speak life to your situation. Decree the blood of the lamb over your family, children, marriage, career, finances etc. You will see the wonder making God manifest His glory in your life.

However, faith goes together with obedience. Abraham obeyed when he was told to leave his nation, people, language—abandoning everything he knew to start afresh to life unknown. The life of faith is an adventurous life. Sometimes you don't even know where you are going as long as God got your back. These are the people of the word. Men and women who obeyed when called. Obey the call of God in your life.

You do much damage in the kingdom of Satan when you make the word of God honorable in your life. Taking the word seriously, prophesy, bible study, fellowship and more. Above all, meditate on the word as it will build up your spirit that will allow you to stand against the wiles of the Devil. Good state of mind comes through the production of the Living Word.

The word of God is the sword of the spirit to silence all the demonic powers that are against you. The wiles and devices of the Devil can be silenced by taking authority of who you are in Christ and say "it is written". This is the same Principe Jesus used to defeat Satan. Three times Jesus quoting the bible, from the book of Deuteronomy "it is written".

What we should learn from Jesus is that He didn't fight the enemy with His own strength but through the power that lies in the very own word of God. We can also do the same as Christians to be grounded in the word to rebuke all the wiles of the Devil 24/7 in our lives. Because the devil does not go anyway. You will have to resist him through the Living word of God.

Matthews {4:4} And Jesus answered him, saying, It is written, That man shall not live by bread alone, but by every word of God.

And Jesus answered and said unto him, Get thee behind me, Satan: for it is written, Thou shalt worship the Lord thy God, and him only shalt thou serve And Jesus answering said unto him, It is said, Thou shalt not tempt the Lord thy God. {4:13} And when the devil had ended all the temptation, he departed from him for a season.

Psalm {19:7} The law of the LORD [is] perfect, converting the soul: the testimony of the LORD [is] sure, making wise the simple. {19:8} The statutes of the LORD [are] right, rejoicing the heart: the commandment of the LORD [is] pure, enlightening the eyes. Psalm119:161-164 Princes have persecuted me without a cause: but my heart standeth in awe of thy word. {119:162} I rejoice at thy word, as one that findeth great spoil. {119:163} I hate and abhor lying: [but] thy law do I love. {119:164} Seven times a day do I praise thee because of thy righteous judgments.

We can also tell from psalms that David was the man of Word and prayer. He will mediate day and night upon the word of God. He will praise the Lord seven times a day. Some of us can't even keep up with that level of dedication to prayer. Moslems prays 5 times a day. Jews prays three times a day. I feel like we as Christians we are slacking when it comes to prayer—we are hot and cold at times. I came across this scripture, and it inspired me and mesmerized me, psalm 119:164 Seven times a day do I praise thee because of thy righteous judgments.

Chapter 4-Bearing much fruits

Psalm 85:11 Truth shall spring out of the earth, and righteousness shall look down from heaven.

You are able to judge if someone walk in truth by examining their character. In other words, character is everything. You will have a very anointed men and women of God doing wonders in the kingdom of God, but one thing that will afford them the fall is undeveloped character. Leadership is all about character—especially godly character that will make impact in the lives of people. When good people lead, the land is healed.

It is the same when you engaging in spiritual warfare, your good standing before the Lord matters. Otherwise the enemy will creep in and assassinate you around the weakling of your character. You cannot be speaking foul with your mouth and expect to reap the fruits of your mouth through proclamations, decrees and declarations. You have to be on the clean slate. We are snared by the words of our mouth. The kingdom of God is the kingdom of Words.

You release your heart faith through your mouth. What's more, your mouth is ordained to speak prophetic words of the Most High—words that will change your life and nations afar.

Psalm 1:2 But his delight is in the law of the LORD; and in his law doth he meditate day and night. 3 And he shall be like a tree planted by the rivers of water, that bringeth forth his fruit in his season; his leaf also shall not wither; and whatsoever he doeth shall prosper.

To sum up this scripture, let the joy of the Lord be your strength. In due time you shall have your heart desires when you delight in Christ.

Psalm 37:3 Trust in the LORD, and do good; so shalt thou dwell in the land, and verily thou shalt be fed. 4 Delight thyself also in the LORD: and he shall give thee the desires of thine heart. 5 Commit thy way unto the LORD; trust also in him; and he shall bring it to pass

Good fruits in your life gives you confidence before the devil because he has nothing to snare you with. The word "Satan" means accuser. He accuses us daily before the presence of God. So, it is through faith that we are going to sail through and silence his claims. The blood of the lamb in the life of a believer rebukes the devil when he accurses us before the very throne of the Most High. Plus, we have the high priest of our new covenant who defend us before the court of the Lord God. Leading a holy lifestyle is the only route.

We can learn one or two from the life of Job—the suffering servant of the Lord. When all calamities hit him hard—he still continued to praise the Lord. Unlike many of us when we go through the most in life, we start to question even the existence of God. For so long we have been sailing on hot or cold faith sometimes. I can understand that life does not throw us roses—we can do a lot more with an unshakable faith. When Elijah on the wilderness thinking that it is the end of the race for him—Jezebel throwing deadly threads on him—the angel of the Lord strengthens him. Likewise, be strengthened in trying times. Imagine the tap of the angel on your shoulder "you still have a long way to go".

You might be going through divorce, you might be going through depression like the man of God Elijah, but cheer up daughter of Zion, For I know the thoughts that I think toward you, saith the LORD, thoughts of peace, and not of evil, to give you an expected end.

Chapter 5- Women of praise

The sword of spiritual warfare is praise! Praise is second handy to the glory of the Most High. The glory come down when we lift up the name of God of Jacob. The king is the king when his followers acclaim his rulership through praise and worship.

It is funny that the Devil wanted Jesus Christ to worship him. He wanted the eternal being—eternal rock of the ages to bow down to His creation. In the beginning there was the Word—Christ. Whatever you worship has total control over your life. If you worship God—He take over your life. Our lives should display an ideal image God has in store for us. We are the children of the Most High through holy spirit sealed in our hearts.

Let us sing holy spirit inspired songs. There is power in worship. God delivered David from all his battles because David's heart was not divided. He had total confidence in the Lord. Yes, he stumbled a lot like some of us do—but he will seek the face of the Lord no matter what. If we can allow God to be the master of our lives, we will go through the storms and come out the other side. We will be like eagles, flying through the storms. The faith walk does not say the journey will be all glossy. No, it is a hard knocks journey. Only those who are bold like lions preserve.

The moment you are in Christ—all hell broke. Satan will be after you till the end of the age. He goes back and forth patrolling the earth looking for whom to steal, kill and destroy. But we have overcome through the blood of Christ. Jesus did. Though we still have to reinforce the victory in our lives. Salvation does not cancel our forefather's generational curses. We have big part to play— like freeing ourselves from the grip of all curses, and close portals that the enemy uses as a legal right in our lives.

Worship can have you tread upon your enemies. David rose up early to praise the Lord. Paving a way for him through the day because he had so many enemies. Early will he seek the Lord.

Awake, psaltery and harp; I myself will awake early psalm 108: 3 David understood that mystery happens through the night and day. He rose up early to command the morning and day. If you can study psalm 91 critically, you will understand that David had enemies everywhere—even in his own family. Besides him being a warrior, he was also a spiritual warfare leader. He dealt with principalities and powers of darkness in his lifetime. We cannot talk about worship and not talk about David.

Psalm 2:2 The kings of the earth set themselves, and the rulers take counsel together, against the Lord, and against his anointed

Behind every king or queen, there is power or force. If it is not the Lord, then is the Devil. Throughout history kings and queen who assumed power, were either under the rulership of God or Devil. This statement talks about the earthly kings and also spiritual rulers behind these kings—the Devil. If you are against the government of God, there is spirit in the background playing through you. The world is spiritual. Nothing happens in this world is coincidence. God is spirit. Everything good or bad happening, is as the results of spirits.

Thus worship is the most important element of the kingdom business. When you worship God, you literally make it known to any kingdom who is your master. God want us to worship him so that He can fellowship with us and elevate us. We draw from His glory when we worship. Diseases flee. Demons flee. And the Devil backs off when we magnify the Lord. Where your loyalty lies—is where your heart is.

Psalm 99:5 Exalt ye the Lord our God, and worship at his footstool; for he is holy.

At the feet of the Lord there is comfort, peace and love. The embodiment of this is Christ Himself. He is the fullness of the Godhead. He is the only one who can step in and out of the unapproachable light of the Father. God is light. God is spirit. God is love. He is the great I AM. He is whatever you need Him to be. Worship only the Lord, and see the wonder making God. Great deliverance comes when you are overtaken or overshadowed by the glory of God. When the glory is upon you, sickness, worry, pain and others go! Glory comes down when we worship and praise the King.

Whenever an evil godly spirit overcame Saul, David would take his lyre and play upon it with his hand. Then Saul was refreshed and relieved, for the evil spirit departed from him (1 Sam. 16:23).

God inhabit the praises of Israel. You are peculiar because you belong in the house of God. In the family of God—the family of all things that are pure. Demons left Saul when David was around. It is the anointing that breaks all kinds of yoke. The beautiful thing about worship is that you don't need to be a good singer. All you have to do is freely open up your heart and sing from there. Sing the holy word of the Living God. Bible is your weapon. You fight through the Word. Walls of Jericho falls when we sing unto the Lord. There is confusion in the camp of your enemies when you magnify the Lord with worship and praise. People, sing psalms to the Lord. Sing psalms to every situation of your life. The Lord is your redeemer. He is still the MAN OF WAR.

Exodus 14:13-14 And Moses said unto the people, Fear ye not, stand still, and see the salvation of the LORD, which he will shew to you to day: for the Egyptians whom ye have seen to day, ye shall see them again no more for ever. 14 The LORD shall fight for you, and ye shall hold your peace.

There one diseases that all mankind are familiar with, and that's fear. Fear has aborted God-given purpose of millions of people all around the world. Fear is the number one weapon the enemy uses to keep us from the very best of God. The is only one way of chasing the spirit of fear out of your life—and that is by dwelling in the secret place of the Almighty God. You shall hold your peace, and fear not.

Chapter 6- Women of faith

Faith is the engine of the heart of every Christian. We have seen many doors shut but when you act with your unshakable crazy stubborn faith to situations—mountains shift. And faith comes as easy as ABC—but many complicate things thinking maybe you need to be more spiritual to exercise the God kind faith. Simply take the word of God with readiness and joy to your heart—faith will spring forth.

The more you chew the word, the high you will stand even in rocky seasons. Women of faith build arks for their families. They patiently snatch their children out of the hands of the devil through supplication and petition unto the Lord. Many followers of Christ were women. Even today, women make up a large number in churches. They double up the number of men in church. From centuries they always knew the power of prayer. It is the seed of the women that will destroy the works of darkness.

Christ gave us the blueprint of how to wage spiritual warfare the right way. And it is through faith that we will overcome the works of darkness. It is the real shield against the wiles of the devil and fiery darts of the enemy.

These are some of the things you can apply to overcome the battle in your life. However, all these requires faith.

The name of Jesus

The blood of Jesus

Confession of the word

Proclamations, praise and worship

Through decrees and declarations

I have won many battles in my life through the power of God. Besides God, you cannot lift even a finger. The finger of judgement will be upon your enemies when you are all fired up for God. The anointing of Elijah is a corporate anointing at this day and age. Both men and women can stand in the office of prophet Elijah.

Elisha stood in the office. John the Baptist also walked in spirit and power of Elijah. This is the spirit of boldness whereby the lion and lioness in you roars through your prophetic works. Faith is bold. Faith talks. And when it talks it talks about everything in line with the word of God.

Chapter 7- Power of fellowship

1 John 1:7 - "But if we walk in the light, as he is in the light, we have fellowship with one another, and the blood of Jesus, his Son, purifies us from all sin."

This verse highlights the importance of walking in the light and having fellowship with one another. When we are honest and transparent with each other, we can experience the purifying power of Jesus' blood and grow in our faith.

Hebrews 10:24-25 - "And let us consider how we may spur one another on toward love and good deeds, not giving up meeting together, as some are in the habit of doing, but encouraging one another—and all the more as you see the Day approaching."

This passage emphasizes the need for believers to meet together and encourage each other in love and good deeds. By meeting together and building relationships with other believers, we can spur each other on and grow in our faith as we await the return of Christ.

Many of us like to be solo-riders. Especially in my family, we are more depended on ourselves. While it is not a bad thing but as believers, the best experience is to share your faith with the world. In the early days of the apostles and believers in Christ, fellowshipping and holy communion were big thing. Now it is a thing of the past. You are more empowered and strengthen when you are around people of the same commonality—which is the love of God.

In times of trying times you will not feel all alone. I am not implying that you make a lot of friends with believers but the community of godly people will inspire you to reach ever high miles in Christ. It just that nowadays people prefer their own space because of hurtful past experiences.

Psalm 147:3 He healeth the broken in heart, and bindeth up their wounds.

As believers in Christ, we were not meant to walk this journey alone. Fellowship with other believers is not only important, it's essential for our spiritual growth and wellbeing. In fact, the Bible tells us in Hebrews 10:24-25, "And let us consider how we may spur one another on toward love and good deeds, not giving up meeting together, as some are in the habit of doing, but encouraging one another—and all the more as you see the Day approaching."

When we fellowship with other believers, we have the opportunity to encourage and uplift each other in our faith. We can share our struggles and victories, pray for each other, and offer support and guidance. We can also learn from each other's experiences and perspectives, and grow in our understanding of God's Word.

Fellowship with other believers can take many forms, from attending church services and small groups to informal gatherings and social events. The important thing is that we are intentionally building relationships with other believers and creating opportunities for mutual support and encouragement.

In addition to the benefits of personal growth and encouragement, fellowship with other believers is also important for our witness to the world. Jesus said in John 13:35, "By this everyone will know that you are my disciples, if you love one another." When we demonstrate love and unity with other believers, we show the world what it means to be followers of Christ.

Of course, fellowship with other believers is not always easy. We may have disagreements or conflicts, or we may feel hesitant to open up and share our struggles. But it's important to remember that we are all imperfect people, and we all need grace and understanding. When we approach fellowship with humility and a willingness to learn from each other, we can create an environment of love and support that strengthens our faith.

In conclusion, fellowship with other believers is a crucial part of the Christian life. It provides opportunities for personal growth, encouragement, and mutual support, and it also bears witness to the world of our love for Christ and for each other. If you're feeling isolated or disconnected, I encourage you to seek out opportunities for fellowship with other believers. Whether it's attending a church service or reaching out to a friend, you'll find that the support and encouragement of fellow believers can make all the difference in your spiritual journey.

Chapter 8- Repentance is king

Psalm 51:1-7 Have mercy upon me, O God, according to thy loving kindness: according unto the multitude of thy tender mercies blot out my transgressions. 2 Wash me throughly from mine iniquity, and cleanse me from my sin. 3 For I acknowledge my transgressions: and my sin is ever before me. 4 Against thee, thee only, have I sinned, and done this evil in thy sight: that thou mightest be justified when thou speakest, and be clear when thou judgest. 5 Behold, I was shapen in iniquity; and in sin did my mother conceive me. 6 Behold, thou desirest truth in the inward parts: and in the hidden part thou shalt make me to know wisdom. 7 Purge me with hyssop, and I shall be clean: wash me, and I shall be whiter than snow.

David understood the power of a forgiven man. Sin separate us from God. While a set apart life from rest draws you near to your Creator every minutes. Holiness grant us access to the face of God while faith make us right standing with God. These are all but mercy and glory of God. It is by the goodness of the Lord that you are forgiven. It is by the mercy of God that you are can come before Him. It is all nothing but the grace of God. We are the children of grace—freely purged by the blood of the lamb. Bought with a priceless blood of the new covenant led by Christ Himself.

When one repents the kingdom of God rejoice. While the other guy is unhappy. It is through holiness that we can get to be in fellowship with God at the end of our days. Repentance is the weapon that silence the demons and nasty spirit that have been living in our temples—our bodies. Demons finds a way to us through legal access established by personal sins or generational sins. So, when we repent we will be able to break all kinds of curses, renounce them and drive demons out eventually.

Repentance is the soldier 's weapon of defence and attack. When you are riding on clean slate with Christ, you can come boldly to the throne of grace with your petition and having confidence that it shall be added unto you. Sin open doors to the demonic attacks. It grants the accuser of our brethren a legal right to wreck our lives to the ground. The Devil does not have love for anyone. Whether be it to his government or his human agents. Don't be fooled when he calls you his son. He will at all-time wage warfare with mankind who resembles the face of the spirit of the LIVING GOD.

I come from a church that was serving Lucifer. I was fooled by majority of following the so called the man of God had. Many of us believers we tend to go by our senses than spirit. There is a difference between natural senses and spiritual senses. There is also a difference between confidence and faith. The greatest weapon of this end age is spirit of discernment. This will save many of us from wandering if it is the voice of God or the devil. These are the two kingdoms in rivalry, the kingdom of God and the kingdom of the Devil.

The two great graces essential to a believer in this life are faith and repentance. These are the two by which grant us the ticket to the eternal life with God. Faith and repentance preserve the spiritual life just as heat and radical moisture preserve the natural. The grace which I am going to discuss is repentance.

Total deliverance is repentance from the sins of our forefathers and our own. When we are under sin the enemy can do what he pleases. The enemy of your heart—the devil will bombard you with host of demonic attack whenever there is access to your soul through sin.

Repentance is a grace required under the gospel. Some think it legal; but the first sermon that Christ preached, indeed, the first word of his sermon, was "Repent" (Mat 4.17). And his farewell that he left when he was going to ascend was that "repentance should be preached in his name" (Luk 24.47). The apostles went on to preach the same message "(Mar 6.12).

Repentance is about gospel grace. The covenant of works allowed no repentance; there it was: sin and die. Repentance came in by the gospel. Christ has purchased us through his blood so that repenting sinners can be saved. The law required personal, perfect, and perpetual obedience. It cursed all who could not come up to this: "Cursed is everyone that does not continue to do all things which are written in the book of the law" (Gal 3.10). It does not say, "He that does not obey all things, let him repent;" instead, it says "let him be cursed." Thus repentance is a doctrine that has been brought to light only by the gospel.

I have always viewed repentance as a warfare against the kingdom of the darkness. The enemy leaves you when you come clean with God. Though he will try you to see if you won't go back to your old ways. Repenting is coming back to your Father's house once again. It is a way of life. Beautiful journey of life is a road of no perfection from our part but from God. God is the cup of our salvation—our robe of righteousness.

You will never lose a fight if you can be the man of repentance. Look at David, through his shortfalls and shortcoming, God was able to restore, revive and forgive him. The life of David is a picture of God's mercy and grace. We do not deserve grace but we deserve mercy. Grace is a virtue from God. Our God is a gracious Lord. Compassionate. Kind.

Biblically we understand that because of the rebellion of the fall of man, we need redemption. Without the renewing of the Holy Spirit, spiritually-speaking, our hearts were corruptible so God had to call us to repent! It can only be the work of God. Humility is the first step to repentance.

"Therefore say unto the house of Israel, Thus saith the Lord God; Repent, and turn yourselves from your idols; and turn away your faces from all your abominations." Ezekiel 14:6

"And saying, Repent ye: for the kingdom of heaven is at hand." Matthew 3:2

"I tell you, Nay: but, except ye repent, ye shall all likewise perish." Luke 13:3

"The Lord is not slack concerning his promise, as some men count slackness; but is longsuffering to us-ward, not willing that any should perish, but that all should come to repentance." 2 Peter 3:9 (KJV)

Chapter 9- Living a fasted life

A fasted life is a life dedicated to the service of God. It is not a command though, but it can turn your life around in a fruitful way. You shall bear much spiritual fruits as you will be planted around the power source of God. There are numerous weapons of warfare God entrusted us with. And prayer and fasting is one of those weapons I call weapons of destruction. Demons cannot stand the fire that is in your body when you have fasted and prayed.

If your eyes can be opened and God shows you your own body, you will be amazed. In the spirit realm it is light that determines how close are we to God. He is not called the Father of Lights for nothing. Through Christ we are the light of the world. Therefore, the light of His countenance falls upon us when we take spiritual things seriously. We are not supposed to be hot and cold, but all time ready for we are the army of the Lord. While Christ leading as the commander of the army.

The fasted life offers you many more in store. Peace of mind, spiritual strength, spiritual revelations and cleansing both physically and spiritually. If you are someone who is struggling to hear the voice of the Holy spirit correctly—fasting is the easiest and cheapest method you can practice. But it is going to be really difficult if you are starting out or if you have not fasted in a long time. You just have to take it easy. It can be intimidating hearing some of friends completing 40 days or 21 days fast while you can't even complete one day.

I believe more than anything, prayer and fasting is an act of humility before the Creator of the universe. Isaiah 58 chapter has a good deal to say about fasting—the correct way of fasting. Biblical and scriptural fast are the only way to total deliverance. Unless you are fasting as a diet.

Fasting has always been the principle of the kingdom of God—a powerful tool or weapon to use in times of trouble. Biblical giants we admire, mastered the art of fasting in their lives. Prayer and fasting has always been like yin and yang—they go together. If you want to move up in ranks spiritually—master the art of fasting while praying. Because fasting itself, it is just a diet or hunger strike if you are not praying. Prayer and fasting dismantle the bonds of wickedness in your life. If your situation is not changing no matter what you do, it is high time you humble your soul with fasting.

Fasting is an act of humility. I have taught a lot about the subject—spiritual warfare. Prayer and fasting is what I emphasis at most to my student in Christ. I know what prayer and fasting can do in the lives of believers. Great men and women such as Jesus Christ, Elijah, Moses, Samuel, David and John the Baptist changed nations in their time with only prayer and fasting. Do you know that the nation of Nineveh was speared of God's wrath because they humbled their soul through fasting in the time of Jonah? Things change in the realm of the spirit when you give God your time and your heart. Fasting and praying is the heart issue.

There is a lot you can lot about fasting. Fasting isn't a hunger strike for faith filled believers, it is an act of drawing near to Him. Because without Him we are nothing. He must increase in our lives and we must decrease. That's how we will walk in spiritual dimension we haven't tapped in. the creative supernatural power of God manifest in our lives when we unlearn ungodly habits and drink from the fountain of uncontaminated knowledge of the Creator.

This can only be the result when you dedicate your life to the will of God—unequivocal submission to the will of Yahushua, Holy spirit and Yahweh. Fasting and praying brings you the result of walking in power and spirit just as prophet Elijah and notable prophets in the bible walked. You can call upon the fire from heaven when you walk in authority, anointing and faith! Yahweh wants His children to experience His glory. He will always reward those who diligently seek Him.

We see in the old testament prophets, kings and people were mourning—renting their heart before God when God was about to bring judgement upon the nation. The nation of Nineveh and king Ahaz are the perfect example. The act of one humbling his or her soul to God is a big thing to God. He is merciful, gracious, kind and compassionate. In this last days—he showed us how much He loves us through His Anointed Son—Christ.

Chapter 10- The power of Meditation

Meditation is an important aspect of everyone who wants to perfectly fellowship with God. Like many of you, I used to shun this practice as I thought it was demonic to meditate. Everything that is done out of the will of God can get us into trouble. Allow God to be the essence of your whole being. We cannot fail to understand that one the pillar of Joshua's success lied in meditation. He meditated day and night upon the laws of God. Isaac meditated during evening hours. King David meditated early in the morning and upon his bed. Christ meditated in the early hours—secluded Himself to fellowship with His Holy Father.

But I also have to say that there is danger to meditation if you don't meditate with the word of God. Anything that you serve other than God is an idol. I was also a victim of this. I would get deeper into meditation— practising what I have read on some mystical books or from so called Christian writers to find myself connected to foreign spirits that I don't even know. The perimeter is to base everything that you do around the biblical principles. You can never go wrong with the word. The Word is the divine weapon of God. There is power in the word as much as there is power in the blood.

The eastern mystic teaching uphold meditation as a way of experiencing inner peace of mind. Indian Gurus regard meditation as the pillar of spiritual growth. This is true. How much more can you go as son and daughter of the Most High when you meditate upon His word and act on it? You can change your life from better to great. We are always called to come up high in spirit of revelation, understanding and wisdom. Apostle John was called to come up high to receive the end time revelation. Prophet Daniel walked in spirit of excellency in all kingdoms because he took the word of God serious. His life has never been the same once he learned from the prophetic books of Jeremiah.

Same as the people during the prophetic times of Ezra and Nehemiah, they have found hidden scrolls in Jerusalem, when the mosaic law of Moses was read for all people to hear—they all wept because they weren't leading their lives according to the status and ordinances of Yahweh. Motivational speakers they can inspire us to achieve set goals in our lives—while the word of God can forever change our hearts. Man can try to inspire you to change your mind. God touches heart. God touched David's heart—from David's soul came beautiful spiritual poetry psalms songs that still touches millions of people still today. God called us to walk the walk of Enoch. Enoch walked with God 300 years. This can only be the walk of faith. He pleased His maker and was granted a prestigious honour in the hall of faith. This is the man who doesn't know the taste of death. If you have ever read the book of Enoch, you will find that Enoch was a messiah of his time. It is he who saw Christ, the redemption of mankind, the last days and great judgement of God.

Enoch was the 7th from Adam. I would like to call Enoch the Founder of faith. Abraham the Father of faith. Noah the preacher of righteousness. We have the cloud of witness as the people of God who we can reference in our godly walk. This is the undying anointing of men and women who became hermits due to the call. From now and then—we should remember and celebrate their lives as the house of God. We are called to the higher calling in Christ.

It all start with the word of God. Observing, meditating and acting on the Word. Christ is the Living Word. When you encounter Christ—you encounter the embodiment of the Word. Even when you reading Torah, or the Old testament, you are still taking a journey on the footstool of Christ Himself. He is the man of Torah. We should also remember that when Jesus was on earth—there was no new testament. The word "testament" is the evidence or proof. It means that when you read the bible, you are injecting the truth of God. It is the truth that set us free.

Meditating on the truth of God will unveil to us who the liar is. Truth mixed with a lie cannot stand. When you read psalm 1—it differentiates between the children of the light and darkness. The godly and the wicked. It all comes to this point that, those who meditate on the word of God shall prosper in all thing. Shall be planted in a garden like fruitful vine trees. Meditate on the word. Meditate on the truth. Truth shall set us all free.

Chapter 11- Women of Prayer

The best way to pray is to pray the scriptures. God answers according to His will. His will is in the bible. Find scriptures that speaks to your situation—declare them, decree them, confess them till they become part of you. All faith ministers I have encountered—will tell you the same thing that faith is engineered by the word. Apostle Paul says "I believe, therefore, I speak". King David also did the same thing. When you believe, you testify about your faith.

There is this great man of God who is asleep now—Derick Prince. I used to enjoy and treasure his teaching about the confession of faith and his testimony about the blood of the Lamb. Many demons have fled from my soul and body through his teaching about the precious blood of the Lamb by just listening to his teaching. The Lord is faithful and his glory is greater and doesn't have borders, barriers or race color. I have been delivered through teaching, singing and also through the word. That's shows you the power of the Word as the divine weapon of God. Remember, The Lord is a Man of war.

Our prayers are weapon of warfare. Our praises are weapon of warfare. Countless of time Christ performed miracles through the gesture of thanksgiving unto the Lord. The Lord values prayers that comes from a sincere heart. Humility is a big thing to the LORD. The mercy of God is greater when we humble ourselves in all kinds of prayers. I cannot limit prayer to one dimension that even to meditate without speaking, it is still an act of prayer.

Reminding God His word is a powerful way of praying. Praying the prayers in the bible of ancient saints, declaring and decreeing the prophetic words of the bible—speaking promises of God to our lives, children, community and nation is the real prayer that would never go wrong in this life, and in the life to come. The Holy spirit ride upon the Word. The overflow of the spirit is the flow of God's will to mankind. It is He that remind us the Word. The Living spirit of Almighty God will always at time point us to Christ.

Chapter 12- Power of Worship

Worship is the language of heaven.

Psalm 148:1 Praise ye the Lord. Praise ye the Lord from the heavens; praise Him in the heights. Praise Him all ye angels; praise him all ye hosts.

God is to be praised in heaven, on earth, in the seas and beneath earth. His ministering spirits in heaven sings of his glory. Every second there are heavenly beings looking at His glory crying unto each other saying "Holy, Holy, Holy" (Isaiah 6:3). When we praise and worship God—we praise for who He is—not what for what He can do for us. He is worthy to be praised by everything that has breath upon the face of the earth.

Psalm 2:3 Thou art holy, O thou that inhabitest the praises of Israel.

The Lord is the King. The kings is worthy to be praised. When we magnify the king—the glory of the king come down on us. The glory is the power and the presence of His spirit.

David is the man after God's heart. He couldn't rest before he sees the ark of the Lord in a proper dwelling place. His life is marked with praises, worships and adoration to the Living God.

Psalm 18:3 I will call upon the Lord, who is worthy to be praised; so shall I be saved from mine enemies.

Paul and Silas were delivered through the power of praise and worship at midnight hours. At your midnight hours lies your deliverance. The Passover of Israelites took place at midnight hour. You will find Christ praying during this times. The Devil is at work during this time—this is a critical time for spiritual warfare.

The kings of Israel and Judah many times were spared through worship. Joshua conquered Jericho through praise. If you want to conquer your obstacles, sing unto the Lord. You don't have be a great singer for the Lord to hear you. All you have to do is to sing in the spirit. God is spirit. The heavenly language is a spiritual language. Heaven is a spiritual place. The atmosphere of heaven is filled with beautiful music of adoration unto the Lord. Give your heart to the LORD. And see the wonders in your lives.

Chapter 13- Prophetic singing

Prophetic singing is different from singing just another gospel song. Or rather a song that inspires you. Prophetic singing is manifesting the glory of the LORD on earth. When you sing prophetically, it means you are inspired spiritually. Most of the time you may hear a song in your heart as a believer, and most of the time we will just shove it off.

The Holy spirit works within the sphere of our hearts, spiritual senses—our body are the carrier of this amazing presence of God. Sometimes the holy spirit may drop something in your thoughts. And you will be thinking is the devil or your own thoughts. It is every believer's ability to develop their discernment when it comes to spirits. I have missed it most of the time thinking it is not the spirit from God, or it is my own thoughts. The thoughts of the Devil are fighting the will of God. You will be able to discern spirits when the word is in your heart. God speaks to hearts. Devil will try to fill your mind with all thoughts that are unscriptural. Everything that bring doubt and fear in your mind is not from God.

There is difference between a holy fear, natural fear and demonic fear. A frequent command given to God's people in the OT is to *"fear God"* or *"fear the Lord."* It's important that we understand what this command means for Christ's followers today. Only as we truly fear the Lord will we be freed from all destructive and satanic fears. By fearing God, we can avoid being trapped by the natural pull toward going our own way, defying God and giving in to the inviting ways of immoral behaviour.

The fear of the Lord is the beginning of the knowledge. Fear of the Lord is righteous while the demonic fear is an attack to our soul to bring us to fruitlessness. Singing prophetic song change the atmosphere of our community. House we live in are dedicated to the Lord when we sing prophetically. Worship breaks limitations. Demons flee. The kingdom of the enemy is turned ups and down when we magnify the LORD.

Demons they don't want to hear the name of the Lord. They tremble when you mention the name of the Lord. Be that generation that will always remember the name of the LORD. Majority remember the LORD when they are in deep waters.

Chapter 14- Declarations and decrees

A decree is an official order issued by a legal authority. YOU are authorized by the living God to walk in power and authority. Man lost it in the garden of Eden but thanks to God for the precious blood of the Lamb that overcame.

A decree is taking God's words and speaking them out. We have been given the authority from Jesus to make these decrees into our realms of influence and as we do it we begin to create the will of God in our life in the spiritual realm.

- Thou shalt also decree a thing, and it shall be established onto thee and the light shall shine upon thy ways. – Job 22:28
- *"God confirms the word of His servant ..."* Isaiah 44:26
- Isaiah 55:11 God said, "My word shall not return void but accomplish all it is sent forth to do."
- "Bless the Lord, you His angels, Who excel in strength, who do His word, Heeding the voice of His word" (Psalm 103:20).

These are prayers for your life and future based on the truths and promises we find in scripture. When we prayerfully decree and declare the Word of God, power is released from heaven in order to manifest biblical promises and blessings in our lives. The Bible says that even the angels harken to the voice of the Word.

As believers, we know that the Word of God is powerful and living and able to bestow life, blessings and abundance. "Death and life are in the power of the tongue." Job 22:28 expresses it this way, "You will also declare a matter, and it will be established unto you; and the light will shine upon your ways." Heaven respond to the word of the Living God. And angels also fellowship with us when we walk in the word. They shall bear you with their hands (Psalm 91).

God's will for our lives is found in the scriptures. Psalm 119:105 says, "The Word of God is a lamp to our feet and a light to our path." The more you study the Bible, the more you will be enlightened. Stories and verses you've known for years will come off the pages as God pours revelation in to your heart and mind.

It is the work of the holy spirit to teach you and impart wisdom as you press in to your relationship with Him through study, worship and prayer. As you continue to spend time in the Word and grow in Him, God will prepare your heart to receive the mysteries of His Word and He'll use it to direct your life.

The word of God will speak to you. You will start being prophetic in your prayers, knowing the will of God and seeing the word manifest before your very own eyes. All you have to do is believe the word and speak the word to your situation. The word has power to change any situation. I have been delivered from demonic oppression by jus confessing who I am in the LORD. The power is in your mouth. Eat your way all the beautiful things through the power of your mouth. Life and death comes through the power of your tongue—you chose.

The power of decrees and declarations

1 . Decrees create and make changes in the Spiritual and Physical Realm

Scripture is a powerful force that creates change in both the physical and spiritual world when spoken.

As you decree God's word and will, the awesome power of the Holy Spirit is released to bring it to pass.

Jesus said the words that we speak are spirit and they are life. The substance of our words goes out into the spiritual realm and starts to creates life.

Remember: "My word shall not return void but accomplish all it is sent forth to do." In order to have what the Bible says, we need to speak it out.

2. Decrees Release and Commission Angels

"Bless the Lord, you His angels, Who excel in strength, who do His word, Heeding the voice of His word" (Psalm 103:20).

Angels respond to the words of life spoken by us. When we speak God's promises and hope into situations, we give these angelic beings something to work with to accomplish God's will and promises in our life.

The moment you decree a thing, it will dispatch angels to go and bring fulfillment to that word of God because they obey the voice of HIS word, not your thoughts.

When you speak His word, Angels are being sent out on your behalf to carry it out. Whether you see a change or not, speaking the Word will ALWAYS do something.

One of the most powerful things you can do to transform your life is to speak and decree certain scriptures into whatever area of life you are struggling with most. Yeah, yeah, yeah..... I know you have heard that a million times but if you knew that it was actually releasing angels and creating changes in the spiritual and physical realm to change your life why WOULDN'T you do it?!

3. Decrees Change Your Beliefs

What you believe about yourself, the world, and your circumstances create your reality.

You create what you believe. Your beliefs control how you perceive life, how you react to situations, what you think about yourself. Whatever your life is now, is based upon your beliefs driving your actions and reactions. We are all perceiving this life completely differently right now based on the filter of our unique beliefs. We need to reprogram our beliefs – so that our habits, personality, ways of thinking, and reactions to life are in line with the people we desire to be.

Declare these prayers over your life.

- My spirit, soul, and body is blessed.
- His hand of grace and blessings is with us and he keeps us from harm.
- The favor of God on my life endures a lifetime and causes my mountains of influence and blessing to stand strong. I am are favored everywhere that I go and in all that I do. His favor opens doors of opportunities for us that no man can shut. Yeshua is a shield to us every day.
- All of my needs are met according to HIS riches and glory by Jesus.
- My prayers are powerful and effective (2 Corinthians 5:21; James 5:16b).
- I am blessed with every spiritual blessing in the heavenly places in Christ (Ephesians 1:3).
- In my home and business, I am the head and not the tail, above and not beneath.

Chapter 15- Women of faith

Bible has so much to say about faith. Faith is a heart issue. You believe with your heart, then you confess with your mouth. Heart and mouth are the important thing in this kingdom. I believe, therefore, I speak. You cannot speak what you don't believe. All the points I have written on this book requires faith. To activate your faith, you have to consume the word of God. Faith comes from hearing the word of God.

You have to believe that the bible is the word of God. And that the word of God is powerful to move away every mountain of your life. Something will not change in your life unless you exercise you God given faith. You study the word. Believe the word. Then speak the word. Confession, declaration, decrees and proclamation are powerful when you speak the very own word of God—the bible.

The unseen realm is more real than this world. This is the place where the universe is controlled. Spirituality affects physical life. Abraham was not only blessed physically but also spiritually. If someone is blessed spiritually even physically he is blessed. Even though he may not realise it. Many of us going through rough life, hardship and lack—sometimes may generational curses following. Salvation cancel our own debt. It does not cancel the transgression of our forefathers.

Majority of us we should stand as intercessor for our own family and family linage before us. This is what Daniel did. Nehemiah and Ezra also so the need to go to the throne of grace for the transgression of the house of Israel and Judah.

Chapter 16- Praying the Psalms

The Psalms are not only great for reading and reciting during times of worship, but *praying the Psalms* is a powerful way to pray Scripture. it is a powerful way to pray because reading the Psalms is like reading a prayer journal filled with the thoughts, feelings, and praises of the psalmists. it is also a great way of expressing our heartfelt emotions and feelings unto God.

The great thing about psalms is that they build you up and increase your prayer vocabulary with right words to say. The best way is to find the psalm that speak much volume to you and personalise it to you.

Psalms were used as a way to worship God through singing and accompanied by musical instrument. I have written a chapter about prophetic singing and worship. Singing to the Lord is the best feeling ever because you don't have to be a great singer—you just pour out your heart to your maker. He is good, and is worthy of our praise! Cultivate sweet communion with God. It calms the turbulent storms in our lives and restores our souls.

Fighting through psalm 91

Psalm 91 is one those psalm that will knock the devil on the floor. You will remember that when Jesus Christ was tempted by Satan, the Devil himself quoted from psalm 91.

Mathews 4:5-7 Then the devil taketh him up into the holy city, and setteth him on a pinnacle of the temple, 6 And saith unto him, If thou be the Son of God, cast thyself down: for it is written, He shall give his angels charge concerning thee: and in their hands they shall bear thee up, lest at any time thou dash thy foot against a stone. 7 Jesus said unto him, it is written again, Thou shalt not tempt the Lord thy God.

I believe the enemy knows the power of psalm 91. Personally, I have seen the power of the Living God through this psalm in my family home that was usually attacked by witches and wizards. Mind you, I am from a well-known village in South African called Mashashane for practicing art of witchcraft. In a place like this, the only survival tool is the word of God.

Psalms have always been my spiritual arsenals. I also had a revelation from God of Jacob that I should sing and meditate psalms each night—and during that season, I have literally seen the hand of God performing wonders in my life. This is a promise to you, you will never go wrong with psalms. Especially this psalm, it will serve as a covering blanket against all sorts of evil agendas.

What I usually do is to personalize each and every psalm to make it my own. And you can also add your own wording to make it more personal. It will literally speak to you.

Psalm 91

1 He that dwelleth in the secret place of the most High shall abide under the
shadow of the Almighty.
2 I will say of the LORD, He is my refuge and my fortress: my God; in him
will I trust.
3 Surely he shall deliver thee from the snare of the fowler, and from the
noisome pestilence.
4 He shall cover thee with his feathers, and under his wings shalt thou trust:
his truth shall be thy shield and buckler.
5 Thou shalt not be afraid for the terror by night; nor for the arrow that
flieth by day;
6 Nor for the pestilence that walketh in darkness; nor for the destruction that
wasteth at noonday.
7 A thousand shall fall at thy side, and ten thousand at thy right hand; but it
shall not come nigh thee.
8 Only with thine eyes shalt thou behold and see the reward of the wicked.
9 Because thou hast made the LORD, which is my refuge, even the most
High, thy habitation;
10 There shall no evil befall thee, neither shall any plague come nigh thy
dwelling.

11 For he shall give his angels charge over thee, to keep thee in
all thy ways.
12 They shall bear thee up in their hands, lest thou dash thy
foot against a
stone.
13 Thou shalt tread upon the lion and adder: the young lion
and the dragon
shalt thou trample under feet.
14 Because he hath set his love upon me, therefore will I deliver him: I will
set him on high, because he hath known my name.
15 He shall call upon me, and I will answer him: I will be with
him in
trouble; I will deliver him, and honour him.
16 With long life will I satisfy him, and show him my salvation.

Fighting through psalm 100

This is my favourite psalm—the gateway to the presence of the Living God. It literally shows you the blueprint of entering into the presence of God through thanksgiving and praise. These two—thanksgiving and praise—declares defeat upon the camp of your enemy.

When you exalt the Lord our God, Satan leaves you. He cannot stand worship. Make joyful songs in your heart and meditate on his goodness. You shall have a new perspective on spiritual warfare. You shall see how small the devil is. The truth is that, whatever you magnify becomes big to your world. Magnify the Lord with your sacrifices of thanksgiving.

The first thing is to pray a thanksgiving prayer. Followed by praise, while praising, bless the name of the Lord. You will automatically feel and sense the presence of the Living king. Then it will be the perfect time for you to make prophetic decrees and declarations.

Psalm 100

1 Make a joyful noise unto the LORD, all ye lands.

2 Serve the LORD with gladness: come before his presence with singing.

3 Know ye that the LORD he is God: it is he that hath made us, and not we

ourselves; we are his people, and the sheep of his pasture.

4 Enter into his gates with thanksgiving, and into his courts with praise: be

thankful unto him, and bless his name.

5 For the LORD is good; his mercy is everlasting; and his
truth endureth to
all generations.

Fighting through psalm 121

Honestly speaking, this is psalm my keeper. Every time I take a trip, this is one of those psalms you have to put in your heart. Even my little sister will call me to check if I had prayed this psalm.

The first talks about lifting up your eyes. It says to all of us, whatever you are in need of, look above where your help is. You don't have to look around you. You will only see your problem bigger and bigger if you look around instead of above where the throne of the Living God is.

You only the beauty of his holiness, the light of his countenance when you look at God. To behold the face of Christ is to look at the invisible God. Christ came as bread from heaven. Bread represent the presence of God. Bread again represent the word of the Living God.

Pray. Meditate. And sing this psalm. The sun and the moon shall not smite you. The evil powers of the day and night shall return void. Testify this beautiful psalm.

Psalm 121

1 I will lift up mine eyes unto the hills, from whence cometh
my help.

2 My help cometh from the LORD, which made heaven and
earth.

3 He will not suffer thy foot to be moved: he that keepeth
thee will not
slumber.

4 Behold, he that keepeth Israel shall neither slumber nor
sleep.

5 The LORD is thy keeper: the LORD is thy shade upon thy
right hand.
6 The sun shall not smite thee by day, nor the moon by night.
7 The LORD shall preserve thee from all evil: he shall preserve thy soul.
8 The LORD shall preserve thy going out and thy coming in
from this time
forth, and even for evermore.

Fighting through Psalm 108

The garment of praise is a heavy load lifter. Your heart is fixed when you sing and praise He who is worthy to be praised. He who inhabits eternity, He who again inhabits the praises of Israel. Get your heart fixed from all anxiety, stress, depression, from all sicknesses of the heart by lifting the lifter of our hearts. God is the restorer and reviver of our hearts beautiful people.

Psalms are songs of deliverance. David sang these psalms seeking God's interventions from trouble. You will likely see from various psalms and the book of prophet Samuel that David spent most his days' unhappy man. This is what happen when you are chosen. Your own family can even disown you. Don't be surprised when things instead of going north going south—hitting the bottom rock.

But at the end of the day, God shall strengthen you—and you shall be a beacon of hope to millions of people all over the world.

Through God we shall do valiantly: for he it is that shall tread down our enemies.

Pray this psalm. Sing this psalm. Meditate on it more and more. It shall speak volume to your life. Your life would never be the same. As someone healed from Schizophrenia through the power of God's Word, without a doubt I can attest that the word of God shall take you from nothing to something. There is power in psalms.

Psalm 108

1 O God, my heart is fixed; I will sing and give praise, even with my glory.

2 Awake, psaltery and harp: I myself will awake early.

3

I will praise thee, O LORD, among the people: and I will sing praises unto

thee among the nations.

4 For thy mercy is great above the heavens: and thy truth rea-

cheth unto the

clouds.

5 Be thou exalted, O God, above the heavens: and thy glory

above all the

earth;

6 That thy beloved may be delivered: save with thy right hand,

and answer

me.

7 God hath spoken in his holiness; I will rejoice, I will divide

Shechem, and

mete out the valley of Succoth.

8 Gilead is mine; Manasseh is mine; Ephraim also is the

strength of mine

head; Judah is my lawgiver;

9 Moab is my washpot; over Edom will I cast out my shoe;

over Philistia

will I triumph.

10 Who will bring me into the strong city? who will lead me

into Edom?

11 Wilt not thou, O God, who hast cast us off? and wilt not

thou, O God, go

forth with our hosts?

12 Give us help from trouble: for vain is the help of man.

13 Through God we shall do valiantly: for he it is that shall tread down our
enemies.

Don't miss out!

Visit the website below and you can sign up to receive emails whenever Johannes Tefo publishes a new book. There's no charge and no obligation.

https://books2read.com/r/B-A-UEZX-SMOIC

BOOKS 2 READ

Connecting independent readers to independent writers.

Did you love *A Women's Guide To Spiritual Warfare*? Then you should read *Youth's Guide To Spiritual Warfare*[1] by Johannes Tefo!

[2]

Deliverance is children's bread. This book is equipped with all the necessary tool you need to be a warrior in the Lord. If youth can grasp this idea of spiritual warfare, they will march all this journey in awareness and readiness to arm themselves all the time for battle ahead.Be equipped with this simple but profound guide that will take you on your next level in your spiritual journey. Having Christ as your commander, you can never go wrong.Add this book to your collection!

---

1. https://books2read.com/u/bryN7Z

2. https://books2read.com/u/bryN7Z

Also by Johannes Tefo

Family spiritual Warfare Books

Generational Curses And Spiritual Warfare: Spiritual Strategies & Principles Of Victory Against Evil Strongholds

Youth's Guide To Spiritual Warfare

A Women's Guide To Spiritual Warfare

Standalone

Deliver Your Soul From Evil

Overcoming Spirit Of Stagnation

The 24: Prophetic Word For This Season 2024 And Beyond

Michael For Warfare

Territorial Spirits: Overcome Evil Strongholds in Your Life And Take Over Your Community With Strategic Warfare And Winning Prayers

Prayers Against Suicide Spirit

Spiritual Warfare When Enough is Enough

Identity In Christ

Prayers Against Satanic Networks

The Workplace You Need: Spiritual Warfare Prayers That Silence Evil Powers At Your Workplace.

Deliverance From Mind Control: Be Free And Delivered From Every Marine Demons Of Mind Control

Times Getting Hard: Scriptures Of Comfort For Hard Days

Battle In The Sea: How To Tackle Spiritual Warfare And Win The Battle

Freedom: Deliverance Of Souls From Captivity

A Dedicated Prayer Lifestyle: Simple Tips To Effective Prayer Lifestyle

Deliverance From Sexual Dreams

Sexual Lust, Demons, And Impurity

Redefined By Fire: Unleashing The Power Of The Holy Spirit Within.

About the Author

Before he started writing Christian books, Johannes got a graduate degree in Film and Television from university of Johannesburg. After that, just to shake things up, he went to equip himself with religious studies, particularly Christianity, just to have knack about the world beyond the curtains of time. And how this body of Christ has transformed millions of people around the world, not neglecting how sadly the movement has been persecuted from time to time. He now writes full time.